WHO ARE YOU TAKING TO HELL WITH YOU?

Scott Johnsen

ISBN 978-1-64468-840-3 (Paperback)
ISBN 978-1-64468-841-0 (Digital)

First Edition

Covenant Books, Inc.
11661 Hwy 707
Murrells Inlet, SC 29576
www.covenantbooks.com

INTRODUCTION

Why This Book

This is a book about the lies and deceits of Satan (the king of lies) and how it plays itself out in the lives of human beings (people). While Satan may deceive us with his lies, there is plenty of truth, evidence, teaching, and guidance on what is the right way and wrong way to react to the ways of this world and our culture and society's grand mistakes.

Our attitudes and our actions lead or point to our beliefs. Unfortunately, these days (possibly these last days), we are not governed by truth, but we are governed by greedy, prideful, confused power-hungry people who have surrendered to Satan and let their emotions guide them instead of truth. It seems Satan works best if he can get you emotionally involved or at least get your emotions to overrule your common sense.

Our emotions fuel what and how we feel about things. If our emotions aren't grounded in fact or truth or sound thinking, we end up with foolish thinking like our confusion on gender, which sounds more like sexual preferences, not genders. Then we have foolish lawmakers and judges passing foolish laws confirming (in their foolish minds) other impossible classes of genders. If this isn't bad enough, then they pass foolish laws forcing those of us who are governed and guided not only by our emotions but also by truth and science to celebrate their foolishness. If we don't celebrate their foolishness, then we are labeled intolerant. The whole while they are the intolerant sect of society, but if they scream loud enough and whine long enough, the squeaky wheel gets the grease, even though it's the weakest and most unstable wheel on the wagon.

Try letting your foolish emotions or feeling guide you on gravity which also is common sense and see how that pans out. Wow! What if some foolish lawmakers try to pass a law saying gravity doesn't exist and they force us to celebrate that also? While you may say that is utter foolishness, only a few short years ago, who would have celebrated all these supposed genders?

God guides us through His word. It's not a mystery or hard to understand. Even someone like me who has worked in construction all his life can understand these simple truths.

Common sense tells us that God created us so then He alone would know what is best for us. Like parents know what is best for their child.

For those of you who think we evolved from some gobbelity goop, really, where is the proof?

To believe that we evolved from a glob of goop spat on to the ground from a molten pond would mean that every plant, animal, bird, bug, fish, mammal, or any other creepy crawly, flying insect, or slithering thing including human beings was all part of this goop. And it began to split and divide to make the mighty redwoods, the king of the jungle, the eagles of the air, and the gigantic humungous whales of the ocean to, name only a few. Oh, and human beings (people). And if that isn't enough, you would have us to believe that for every species of anything that there is, a copart had to evolve perfectly to compliment it so that they could come together and/or unite their own seed and fertilization technique to continue the procreation of each and every species.

Now if evolution wasn't hard enough to believe before, that really puts it out there. I wonder how many zeroes are behind that number for those odds.

In a sense, this book is about choices! We all get them. Some of us choose to let our choices be restricted by the influence of others around us. Some of us are given way too many choices way too early in life. Some of us had the choices of others inflicted on us and have had no choice other than how we respond or react to those wrong choices of others. Some of our choices are from the goodness of our hearts, and some of our choices are from the pride and greediness that live in each and every one of us.

Our choices direct us onto the path we will take. Some of our choices lead us on a path to do what is good, right, and rewarding. Some of our choices lead us on a path to do what is bad, wrong, and restricting. Restricting meaning in the earlier years, a pop on the diaper or a time-out. In the teenage years being given detention or grounded. In the adult years, prison.

We are all given choices, and the choices we make are directly related to the people who had influence over us throughout our lives, with their choices. We have good and bad influences bombarding us daily. TV programs and commercials, celebrities, sports figures, politicians, parents, other family members, teachers, friends, acquaintances, bosses, and coworkers. All these people influence our choices, and we in turn influence the choices of others. So we need to consider the choices we make very carefully and base them not only on how they make us feel but also the truth and why we did consider or make this choice. What is my belief behind this choice? How will this choice influence those around me? Will this choice influence others? And if so, is this for good or for bad?

When God created us, He gave us free will or choice. He gave us the ability to choose. To choose right from wrong and good from evil and any other choice you can imagine.

While animals are for the most part driven by instinct, we are able to hear, see, smell, taste, touch, and reason to make informed decisions or choices, which is why we are and will be held accountable for the choices we make and how our choices will influence our culture, society, and those around us.

About twenty years ago, a young friend of mine made a choice to ask me the most important question I have ever been asked. He asked me if I died right now and was standing before Jesus Christ and He asked me the question, "Why should I let you into heaven?" What would I say? I answered because I am a good person. My friend shared with me that that was a wrong answer. He shared with me that the Bible teaches that none of us deserve to be in heaven with God for all eternity. He shared with me the fact that Jesus Christ who is God allowed Himself to be the sacrifice for all sins for all humanity for all times. That because He in perfect obedience to the will of His father allowed Himself to be beaten, have His flesh torn open, ridiculed, humiliated, and spit on, and then nailed to a wooden cross and while hanging there have a spear thrust into His side, because He shed His blood for my and your sins, that only in accepting Christ's suffering and sacrifice on the cross and desiring to live a life surrendered to Him is there any hope of salvation.

I in my way of thinking from the influence I had in my life and the decisions and choices I had made for the past forty-five or so years thought that I was good enough for heaven. I wasn't bad, I haven't murdered anyone, I didn't cheat on my wife, I worked hard, I went to church sometimes, I paid my bills, and my choices were OK. But I didn't see all the wrong choices I had made and continue to make. I am a sinner, you are a sinner, that person or people you idolize and blindly trust are sinners, those politicians we vote into office are sinners, and every one we allow to influence our choices and decisions are sinners. All of us deserve an eternity in hell separated from God and all that is good, right, and just. We all need a savior. True Christianity is the only faith that teaches you can't do it. You can't be good enough. You can't recite enough prayers. You can't give enough money to your church or organization or accomplish all the traditions or jump through all the hoops your religion tells you you have to do to earn heaven.

God tells us we can't do it. We are all sinners and fall short of the glory of God. When God says all, He means all. Your pope, your pastor, your prophet, the head of you faith, or the one with influence over what you believe whether religious or not can't do it. Each and every one of us need a savior. Again, it's a personal choice you have to make. Your mama or your grandma ain't gonna get you in. It's your heart and your head and what choices you make concerning the grace of God and the sacrifice of His Son, Jesus Christ, that leads to your eternal (which means forever and ever and ever) destination.

Many people don't or won't believe in God, let alone a savior, which is maybe why we have so many different beliefs and religions. We, in our imminent wisdom, want to control our own destiny. Well, congratulations, you are maybe controlling your destination to hell for all eternity (that is forever and ever and ever) separated from God and all that is good, right, and just, which leaves all that is wrong, evil, and unjust.

Maybe that is why so many people choose evolution. They don't want to be governed by a higher authority or held accountable for what a follower of Jesus Christ would call their sins. And in writing this, maybe they are right, if we look honestly at our society and culture today, we do appear to be evolving, only not how they think. We are making decisions and choices based off of emotion and instinct like animals, not from the informed decision-making and reasoning skills God gave us as human beings.

I should end the introduction here because as you can probably tell, and my wife and kids can attest to you that I have an ability to ramble on…a bit. But one more thing.

God doesn't want religion. He desires a relationship. Him being our creator and the creator of the heavens and the earth and everything seen and unseen is like a parent-child relationship. He is the parent, and we are His children. He knows what is best for His children unlike us who think we may know what is best for our children based off of the influences that we allow to govern our choices that we impose or sometimes inflict on the lives of our children.

I pray that you continue to read on and that this book will have a positive influence on the choices you make and influence others with.

I pray that you would consider deeply the title of this book, *Who Are You Taking to Hell with You*, and seek the truth and evidences of how we got here and where we are going.

CHAPTER 1

It's God's Way, Not Our Way
Romans 10:8-15 NLT

When I was about twenty-seven years old, I would say foolish things. For example, when I drive by the church my mom attended, it was like driving through the corner of God's eye, just to let Him know that I was still around. Or even worse, if I go to hell, I'll have lots of friends there with me.

It's not that we were bad people. In fact, for the most part, we were good worldly people. We took care of our worldly responsibilities. We worked, paid our bills and taxes, raised our children up knowing worldly right and wrong, and maybe even helped the needy sometimes.

I would help others when I could or when the opportunity would arise. In fact, I would mow my grandpa's lawn and another elderly couple that I was friends with almost every week during the summer months. Doing good was easy for me.

I was raised by my wonderful parents and was close to my wonderful grandparents on both sides, which meant lots of aunts and uncles of a couple generations, with lots of cousins.

I was the third oldest of our generation with two sisters older than me and one sister younger than me. We were all about twelve months apart. Our younger brother came along around five years after my younger sister.

We were all raised on a forty-acre ranch in Turlock, California. I didn't know it then, but it was the most wonderful place on earth. It was very special and still is today even though we no longer own it. Mom and Dad raised us there with the help of grandparents and other relatives and even friends and neighbors when necessary.

I always thought that the way I was raised was the way everyone was raised. Until I grew older and began seeing and understanding how many other people had been raised with some of the terrible things that they had to endure in their childhoods, which explains so many of the horrible things that happen in our society and culture today.

Bad things don't get better if we do nothing about them. They just grow and multiply, kind of like our national debt (which is another chapter). If we don't seek out help, the right kind of help, things just keep getting bigger and bigger and worse and worse, and pretty soon, they become unmanageable (again like our national debt), and drastic changes become necessary or the only way to start to correct the atrocities that have become commonplace in our culture and society today. If we continue to surrender and give in to self-centered unwise leadership, whose only motivation is what's in it for me, things will continue to grow and multiply, and judgment and punishment become the only possible answer to correct these atrocities.

You are probably thinking that this sounds more like an autobiography or an older man reliving memories or, if you read long enough, a crazy old man ranting and raving about how messed up things are, which you wouldn't be entirely wrong. I have no idea of what I'm doing, except that something in my mind is leading me to do it. I believe it to be the Holy Spirit.

For clarification, it's not an audible voice saying do this or else. It's persistent thoughts that keep coming back. I'm not sure if I'm taking the right action, but I do know for sure that if it is God's leading and I follow in obedience, He will make it happen for His glory.

Two weeks ago at church, our pastor challenged us to sit quietly with God and listen. I try to read my Bible and pray every morning, but I wasn't much for being quiet and listening. So I started first, before reading and praying, being quiet. After a couple days, a title for a book came to my mind, *Who Are You Taking to Hell with You*. Now that's not the first book title I've ever had come to my mind. In fact, I've written down lots of them, but it's the first one that kept coming back. Then I started thinking about the importance of the title, because so many people think they are good people and are going to spend eternity in heaven, when in all reality they are worldly people destined for eternal punishment in hell, even though they may be religious, which is why the title of this first chapter is God's Way, Not Our Way. It is the most important chapter. It is up first, in case you can't stand reading any longer. Hopefully it will make a difference in your and the people that you have influence over eternal destination.

It is important first and foremost that you yourself are reading or begin reading the word of God. Satan again is the king of lies, and the Bible is the word of truth which exposes or shines light on his lies. Satan would have you believe that hell is only for terrible people like murders or rapists or child molesters, the Hitlers or Saddam Husseins of the world, when in all reality, hell will be full of good people. While heaven has degrees of rewards, hell has degrees of punishment. So while maybe you didn't murder anyone, you, like every single one of us, are a sinner. The Bible teaches that none is good, not even one. The Bible teaches that we all are sinners and fall short of the glory of God. The bible teaches that God, in His holiness, cannot be in the presence of sin. The Bible teaches that because of sin, just one single sin, we are not worthy of heaven and are destined for hell. Now you may think I'm not bad, but I'm sure you have had at least one bad thought in your life or said one bad or unkind word. Oops, to late, your hell bound!

Satan would have you to believe that because you're not to terrible, you're OK and you're headed for heaven. Satan even deceives some religious people into believing that they are going to heaven, when all the while some of their beliefs and traditions and practices are an affront to God. Even some people whom would call themselves Christians yet are led by their emotions to condone or even promote practices and ways of life that are very much against the teaching you learn from reading the word of God. Lots of people say that a good God wouldn't send people to hell. The truth is that a loving God won't force you to live in heaven with Him against your will for all eternity. You get to choose.

If you choose Satan and his lies which lead to eternal punishment in the lake of fire or hell, then keep on living the good worldly focused life you are living. You are on the broad road with countless others linked arm and arm to judgment and punishment in hell.

If you choose God and His narrow path to eternity in heaven, then we must understand that it's His way, not our way. The sad thing is that while many, if not most, good people choose either to think they are or can do or be good enough through a check and balance way of thinking or don't think or care about it at all, they are still on the broad road to eternal punishment in hell.

God's word teaches that we can't and don't have to do it. He in His love for us has done it for us. All we have to do is believe and trust in Him and what He has already done for us and repent of our sins and accept His amazing grace! You might wonder why He would do that for me. The answer is He is God, and He created you and loves you. But again, having created you and all that is seen and unseen in heaven and on the earth, He alone knows what is right and best for His creation.

But we as "enlightened" human beings think for our own selfish and self-serving reasons, with our unholy and immoral attitudes and emotional thinking that there is no God or that we know more than He does. So we continue wondering about lost, perverting all that is good, right, and just. We are foolish enough to believe that we can take the wonderful and beautiful gifts that God has so graciously blessed us with and pervert them and that in our confusion and our perversion, there will be no consequences for our horrible sins.

While God's mercy does not give us what we truly deserve, there are most certainly consequences for our sins. All someone has to do is look around and see and listen to the utter foolishness that is everywhere to realize that sin and unrighteousness are running rampant in our culture and society. For example, sex outside of marriage may lead to pregnancy. Pregnancy may lead to an abortion. Abortion leads to the murder of innocent lives. And man's way to fix man's sins: pass laws to protect the guilty and not the innocent.

Let's look at a few examples or explore a few already mentioned. Let's start with gender confusion since it is so in our faces nowadays.

First, remember that I'm not a writer or a researcher. I'm just someone who listens to the news and reads the word of God.

It's my understanding that nowadays, there are more than just two gender groups. I understand also that occasionally, there may be a third group because of a birth defect, which is not my concern here. My concern truly also is not with the other made up or manufactured gender groups of people. My concern is why the so-called leaders of our society and culture feel it necessary to force the rest of us to recognize and celebrate the lifestyles these small percent of people have chosen to live. Again, because I do not agree with their choices does not mean I hate or wish they didn't exist. I just don't believe it is right for a man, who today may feel like a woman, to go into the same public bathroom or shower at a school or gym as my wife, daughter, granddaughter, sister, or any other decent modest woman. I fear for the things that could and have happened in the name of gender equality, when it is not equal at all. I have heard it said on the news that about 10 percent of the people choose an alternate lifestyle. I have also heard it on the news that it is truly closer to 1 or 2 percent that have chosen these lifestyles. So why are the vast majority of us forced to not only recognize this confusion but also celebrate it and live with the new and unjust and immoral laws passed by our so-called political leaders? What happens when they start to pass laws to make it OK to molest children and rape women? They have already downgraded them from violent crimes. Will they then force us to celebrate that also? Will a baker be financially ruined and put into jail because he refuses to bake a cake for someone celebrating their first molest of a young child or rape of your daughter or son?

I must assume these politicians and judges and people who promote and push and force these ungodly lifestyles on the rest of us have no children or families or at least think they are somehow immune from the horrific consequences of the terrible and immoral choices they have made and are making and forcing on our society and culture today.

While they or their family members may escape devastation, destruction, and harm while alive, there will be a price to pay for their arrogant and flagrant and immoral sins. And again the souls they may have led astray because of their willingness to do the work of the devil with the influence they were entrusted with. This is not to say that everyone who succumbs to their immoral influence will not also pay a price for their sins, only that their price may be multiplied.

While Hitler killed millions of Jews in his failed attempt to exterminate their race and others who refused to embrace his socialist type of government, many were not condemned to hell for all eternity, because they believed what the Bible taught about Jesus Christ and had trusted in Him and His sacrifice for their salvation and eternal destination. While these willing participants in Satan's plan may have killed millions of people, I would believe that millions of them were followers of Jesus Christ and therefore are now in heaven, awaiting the second coming of our Lord and their new resurrection bodies.

While these monsters murdered millions, what about the millions of babies murdered by abortion in our country alone every year? Where do you, who not only promote and perform abortion but pass laws to protect the murdering of these innocent souls, think you stand before our great God of justice? You may justify your promoting, performing, and protecting abortion by saying it's a woman's right to choose or that you want it to be safe for the woman, not in some back alley abortion place. Well, if you take an honest look at the evidence and what is happening and the woman who have complications and even die from your so-called safe clean places, you would see just how wrong you are and always have been. Now, while some of these women and their boyfriends or husbands or acquaintances would have sought out an abortion no matter what, many, if not most, would have chosen to give birth and kept or put their child up for adoption. But you have promoted and passed laws to not only make the murdering of babies but also sometimes their mothers who are often children themselves legal and readily accessible, and you continue to pass laws to protect, promote, and profit from this ungodly act. When you pass and promote laws that are contrary and in conflict with what the Bible teaches us about the will of God, you are doing the work of the king of lies, and there will be terrible consequences to pay individually and corporately as a nation if we continue down this unholy path of unrighteousness.

Will you, as someone who promotes and/or passes laws to protect and make these horrible acts against God profitable be held accountable for your unrestricted influence over these mothers who are in need of wise counsel, comfort, and love, not the perversions of this society and culture that you helped make?

I heard someone talking and teaching from the book of Revelation in the Bible, and they said something about the United States not being mentioned in the book of Revelation or the study of end times. They mentioned that maybe it was because of the rapture of the church and the United States was no longer a major power. While this may or may not be true, the scripture doesn't tell us. It may also be because of our promotion of ungodliness and our dedication to promoting and profiting from gross and immoral sins like abortion and gender confusion, and our destruction of godly marriages and the family, along with our unremorseful lifestyles, that our just God found it necessary to punish us as a nation for our own good. No one knows yet!

Now you may think I sound like someone who thinks he is perfect or better than others, but your thinking couldn't be farther from the truth. Like you, I am a sinner. Maybe the difference between you and me is that I hate my sins. I don't promote my sins. I seek forgiveness for my sins, sometimes moment by moment. I don't protect my sins. I repent or turn away from my sins. I don't profit from my sins.

There will be a price paid for my sins and for your sins. Again our differences also may be in payment of those sins. I have trusted and repented and placed my faith in Jesus Christ and Him alone and His suffering and His sacrifice on the cross for the payment of my sins. Seeking forgiveness for our sins is the starting place.

If you are living a lifestyle contrary to the teaching of the Bible, can you truly be seeking forgiveness? If you kiss your sin goodbye every morning and hug your sin when you get home every day and crawl into bed with your sin every night, can you truly hate your sin? If you promote and protect a lifestyle contrary to the teaching of the word of God, you cannot be seeking forgiveness.

It is not to say all Christians don't struggle with their sins. We all do, but when we sin, we don't justify our sin, but we seek forgiveness. When we sin and are punished for them, we don't blame God or others; we turn to God and seek help and guidance and strength to turn from those sins. We don't pass worldly immoral laws to make those sins acceptable and profitable.

Satan has fooled so many of you into believing that just because you feel it is right, it is OK. Charles Manson must have felt it right to murder Sharon Tate and her unborn baby, and you call him a monster.

Nowadays, there are many sad excuses for so-called doctors and sad excuses for so-called leaders and sad excuses for so-called politicians and sad excuses for so-called judges and sad excuses for so-called lawyers murder and pass laws to protect and profit from the murder of full-term babies. You now make it legal to take these born-alive babies into a room and snap their necks or shove a pair of scissors into their unprotected spines. All the while justifying your horrible sin, saying it's what's best for the woman, or it's her right to choose. I bet most of these women are teenage girls who are confused and terrified and in desperate need of guidance, direction, compassion, and godly love, not some sick sad excuse for a doctor looking at a few hundred dollars for a procedure and whatever he or she can get from the sale of baby body parts. You, people, are the true monsters. And we corporately as a foolish and immoral nation continue to vote many of you, monsters, into your dens of wickedness so you can continue to murder babies and destroy the lives of so many of these young would-be mothers and fathers. In your misguided and immoral logic, you have denied many of these women, young and older, to get a glimpse of what God feels with His children, not to mention the traumatic effect on their bodies. You say that many would have given the baby up any way and maybe so, but they would have had an opportunity to use the godly wisdom God had given them if not for your lack of wisdom and your blatant and disturbing promotion of such horrific and immoral sins.

I keep trying to figure out or understand what the end game of such unbelievable foolishness is. Doctors who take an oath to protect life but kill innocent lives and judges, lawyers, politicians, and voters condoning and protecting such immoral wickedness, all the time trying to protect the rights of DACA kids and passing laws to protect your/our pets and animals. How do they, in their minds, justify such stupidity? Again, do they believe that they will not have a horrific price to pay when their time of judgment comes when they stand before the judge of all eternity?

History is full of examples of what happens to cultures and societies who continue down the paths of such degradation and flagrant evilness. They cease to exist. They become a footnote in the chronicles of what has happened repeatedly throughout history.

The amazing thing is that each previous culture and society, just like our culture and society, has had the evidence of the past catastrophes of these no longer existing cultures and societies, and yet we are headed to our own extinction because of our inability to learn from others' mistakes and our own selfish pride, greed, self-righteousness, and immorality. When will people ever learn?

If evolution is true, you would have thought we would be capable of evolving enough to learn from our own mistakes. But society after society continues to crumble, and destruction is inevitable, because we are self-centered, self-absorbed, self-prompting human beings who want what we want when we want it and don't care who has to suffer or pay a price so we can get it.

If you are angered by what I have written, I understand because I to get angry and defensive when someone confronts me with my sin. I feel a need to justify my feelings, my emotions, my choices, and my actions I have taken. But when I sit quiet and listen to my heart, I recognize the wrong things I have done and desire greatly to be forgiven and once again find the peace that comes only in our great God's mercy and grace. Our only hope is surrender and obedience to our great and faithful and unchanging God, who knows what is best for His children.

My prayer is for this nation to once again, like at its founding, become a nation focused on God and His provision. I pray for all of us who have been deceived by Satan's lies that we would find peace, forgiveness, direction, and joy in the arms of our loving King and Creator, Sufferer, Savior, Comforter, and Guide. That your, my, and our God would protect us from the lies and deceits of Satan, from the ways of this wicked world, and our own sinful flesh. I pray that my and our God would open our eyes to His truth, our hearts to accept that truth, and our minds to walk out His truth moment by moment in our daily lives. I pray for a true and genuine salvation in each and every one of our lives.

Thank You

I Love You
Scott

P.S.

In case you have hopefully decided to read to this point and are not sure if something you are doing is a sin, find your Bible, knock the dust off of it, and open to the book of Romans and start reading at chapter one.

CHAPTER 2

Knowledge and Intelligence without Godly Wisdom Are Only Opinions

Well, if you are still reading, welcome to another dose of common sense, and many of you are probably really pissed off. If you remember, I mentioned before that I'm no learned scholar or esteemed person of higher learning. I would say education, but there is so little of that going on nowadays. I don't have some PhD in anything, and I'm surely not a so-called reporter. Because so many of them nowadays make up what they want or feel should be said instead of reporting the facts like they used to do when character and truth meant something.

Nowadays, what I want and feel goes. No matter if it is true or right, it's what I want and feel, and that's all that matters, so that's what I'll print to hopefully mislead the uninformed or ignorant people to what I feel is right no matter what.

I write not based off of what I feel but what I see, hear, and read. I see the things going on, and I can't help but get confused and angry and want to lash out. But I know writing lies, and trying to destroy people because I disagree with them is not the way God intended it to be.

Besides, I know that He will be the final judge on all of our earthly lives, which for me and the way I feel is a big relief. I can let go of my anger knowing that all the lies, stupidity, injustice, and moral degradation, and did I say stupidity inflicted on us, by the so-called intelligent and knowledgeable people will have their day in court. Maybe not here and now in front of their peers but in front of the judge of all eternity who knows the secrets of their hearts and everything they ever thought, said, and did.

When they stand before our great God of justice, I wonder if all the babies they killed will flash before their eyes. I wonder if all the young children they harmed by forcing teachers to teach not only ungodly and unspeakable but totally unnecessary things like their version of sex education to children as young as kindergarten, solely to promote and further their immoral views and life styles, will pass through their minds at their moment of judgment. I wonder about all the teenage girls who had abortions because intelligent and knowledgeable people and lawmakers and judges passed laws forcing teachers to take these children to get an abortion instead of trying to comfort them and help them to understand and share their struggle with their own families. Will all these young lives possibly destroyed by their unjust and immoral actions pass before them as they stand in view of true justice? Will those who pervert God's institution of marriage and destruction of the family, in a failed attempt to justify their own sinful and lustful desires of the flesh, understand or care about God's justice?

How about all the young adults who are misled into believing that the only way they can amount to anything is by going to college and incurring mountains of debt and sometimes walking away, leaving that burden for the rest of us to take care of, and all the while being indoctrinated by all the so-called intelligent and knowledgeable professors who lead them astray doing the work of Satan? You would think that if they were so smart, our society and culture wouldn't be so confused and easily misled and continue down the same road to ruin as all the civilizations before us and even ones in our recent history. Heck our society and culture can't even tell the difference between boys and girls. I guess that's where godly wisdom comes in.

I do believe college has its place. I want my doctor to know about the human body and how it works and my surgeon to be skilled and practiced at his chosen profession. Mostly, I would want them to have a heart to be good and honest and do what's right for the care of their patients. I wonder what kind of schools are turning out so-called doctors who believe it is OK to rip babies piece by piece out of their mother's womb. What kind of teaching are they getting from these so-called intelligent and knowledgeable professors?

I also would like the engineer who calculates bridges and buildings and other things to be taught at higher levels of learning. But it seems like so many of them with their degrees feel they are so much better than the rest of us or at least the rest of us who don't have letters behind our names. A degree is only a degree. It may show how smart you are, but it does not measure your wisdom or your character. What happens after you get the degree shows whether you have wisdom and character or if it has escaped you and your higher education and learning.

I wonder what schools are turning out our judges these days. They seem to feel it is OK to make up their own laws and rules and regulations, instead of following the ones that our founding fathers set up in our constitution to protect us from our own government becoming too powerful and intrusive into our daily lives. They probably went to the same schools that so many of our politicians went to. I guess they feel that because they are so intelligent and knowledgeable, the rest of us are too stupid or ignorant to make it through a day without them telling us how to act or feel, what to do, or where to go or not to go or believe or not to believe. It's amazing we don't forget to breathe without them.

I wonder where these people learned economics, which I think is a fancy or shorter way of saying adding, subtracting, multiplying, and dividing. They sure don't seem to be very good at figuring. Any unintelligent or unknowledgeable person like myself can figure out the following scenario. If you keep adding nontaxpaying people to an already exploding deficit, multiplying the interest on that already engorged deficit, and as older taxpaying people begin to retire or die, subtracting from your tax revenues and not being replaced by a new work force or tax revenue base, because they are all too smart or too lazy to get a real job, and not one that is manufactured by the government at some level which only adds to the deficit, this means that you are now dividing that multiplying deficit among fewer people, which also means higher taxes for the fewer people and less money for their families. Sooner or later, we will get sick, tired, die, or give up and become one of your nontaxpaying creations. Now if I went too fast or made it too simple for you, intelligent and knowledgeable people, let me know, and I'll go over it again only slower this time.

It's not rocket science. You give to those who not only don't earn it but also don't deserve it, and you tend to upset those of us who you continually steal it from. We don't mind helping the needy. But your definition and my definition of needy are two very different definitions. In my definition, I mean widows and orphans and maybe people or families where tragedy has struck and for a period of time may need help to get back onto their feet, not generations of families you allow to abuse the system. The terrible thing is that we who earn our money don't have enough to do much giving or helping of truly needy people because we are forced to pay higher taxes because of your definition of needy, which evidently means any person who doesn't feel like or care to earn a living or is too lazy or too burned out to keep a job and all too often pass down their give me mentality to the next generation. This also means any person from any country who wants to come here to the land not of opportunity but the land of free handouts. I know people who work the system so they don't have to work, and they seem to have more than me. Unfortunately, what you don't give them with all your tax-funded giveaway programs is self-worth. I don't mean self-importance like you see from so many Hollywood and music people and sports figures these days. I mean value in ones' self. Your worth that gets you up in the morning, whether you feel like it or not. Gets you out the door on your way to your job to work in such a way to honor God and to earn a check to pay for your needs and the needs of your family. And prayerfully a little leftover to help the truly needy.

I remember quite a few years ago when the intelligent and knowledgeable and dare I say enlightened members of congress and the president at that time thought it would be a good idea to make it possible for people to acquire a house at little or no cost. They approved people for loans who didn't qualify for small houses, let alone the great big three-car-garage houses they were seeking to buy. They were approving bad loans to get people into houses they truly could not afford. I heard someone say or read somewhere that the idea behind it was that the people would be proud and work harder to keep the American dream of owning a home like previous generations before them. But instead, they made it too easy to fill those three-car garages with fancy high-priced cars, boats, and other unnecessary if unaffordable toys. I also heard or read that the reason why it failed so horribly was because it was made too easy. No one had to work hard and save for a down payment or had to actually qualify for a loan and work hard to have and to keep a good credit rating like previous generations did.

There is not pride in something if we don't have to earn it. And I don't mean inflated ego pride like we see in all too many people today.

A while back, I was flipping channels on my TV, and I came across some kind of award banquet on one of those channels about Hollywood and the famous or, in some cases, infamous people. Talk about your inflated egos and self-importance, my goodness, anything to draw attention to their self. One lady had four dresses she kept peeling off until she finally ended up slithering on the steps of wherever they were at in her underwear! And there were many wearing outrageous outfits. I bet if you added up all the money spent on all of those outrageous and sometimes hideous outfits, you would have millions of dollars. While I realize this may only be a drop in the bucket to them, if they truly cared about the immigrants, the homeless, and the DACA kids like they claim to in some of the things they say, that money could have went a long way to helping and making themselves look a lot less ridiculous. While I have not heard these people claim to be esteemed people of higher learning, they are products of a society and culture that have been bombarded and inundated with a self-serving, all about me way of thinking, and it has to start somewhere.

When you take prayer and godly wisdom out of schools, something is going to take their place. Now we teach two plus two doesn't have to equal to four. As long as you can show how you got your wrong answer, you are still right. Now we teach about perverted sex to kids as young as kindergarten, and if parents want to opt out, their children may become wards of the state and put into foster care. And I wonder what happens to teachers who refuse to teach such obscene unnecessary filth, will they be fired and lose their income for doing the right and proper thing? Will they lose their homes because they refuse to condone such filth and continue the chain of unbridled immortality? I wonder if their unions will stand behind them and strike if necessary to keep them from having to spread more muck and filth on this downhill slide our culture and society have so readily embraced. I wonder how many school board members and school administrators and teachers feel all the sick and disgusting things being taught at school are OK because they too were indoctrinated by the immorality of the intelligent and knowledgeable people teaching them. I wonder if they feel any remorse or guilt when they fire or at least try to fire a male teacher who has enough wisdom to refuse to keep an eye on, I believe, a middle school age girl who feels like a boy and wants to shower with them. The way I heard it, the school wouldn't allow the teacher to inform the parents of the boys that a girl would be showering with them, let alone inform the parents of the girl that she wanted to or would be showering with the boys. I don't know what ended up happening with the teacher, the girl, the boys, or the parents of any of them (i.e., if they ever found out). How does this happen? In whose mind is this OK? What unintelligent and unknowledgeable sick person, people, school authority, judge, politician, or leader of any group would condone such idiotic disturbing and unwise behavior? Again, where do they see this going? Rape, child molestation, and shower sex between two consenting children on school property facilitated by the enlightened learning they are promoting and forcing on the unsuspecting innocent children and their parents who they keep in the dark.

I wonder who thinks this crap up! I know that there are and always have been sick and disturbed individuals, but when they can pervert whole sections of society and especially the so-called intelligent and knowledgeable sect to buy into their sickness, where does that leave the rest of us not so bright people? Out of hell for all eternity, possibly that's where!

That's not to say that only by not buying into the wisdomless people who create and promote such idiotic foolishness are you bound for heaven but that possibly darkness is giving way to light and your eyes are beginning to open to the ways and craftiness of the devil. There is hope for anyone and everyone until your dying breath, the last beat of your heart, and your last conscious ability to repentantly cry out to Jesus Christ for forgiveness of all your sins and to place your faith for all eternity in Him and Him alone.

One of the truly scariest realities is that even institutions of higher learning that are supposed to teach and prepare pastors and preachers have been infiltrated by professors who teach what they feel and not what the Bible says. Or maybe they teach the parts of the Bible they may agree with but not the truths of the entirety of the Bible. When you read about the Bible and why we should trust its teaching, you will find out that it was written over a period of around fifteen hundred years by forty different authors, from three continents, in three different languages, and does not contradict its self like so many other books that religions base their faiths upon. There are hundreds of predictions, and many have come true and many are yet in our future. It teaches about cities and kings that only recently have been discovered. It teaches things about science, the sun, moon, stars, and seasons and how everything came to be. The Bible teaches about people and how we should behave and act and also react to the sins that seem to overwhelm and control our ways of thinking and our lives to the point of apparent ignorance and stupidity.

Let's see what intelligent and knowledgeable people evidently believe based off of the things they say and do and the laws they pass and things they teach.

1. To date, there are sixty-three genders.
2. Marriage is for anyone and anything anytime and as many as you want (maybe not yet but it's coming).
3. Children, as young as possible, should be taught not only about sex but also about their perverted views of sex.
4. If you are born a boy but feel like you're a girl today (so maybe you can shower with them) and then two hours

later again feel like you're a boy, we will pass laws to give you that right, not pass laws to protect girls you have and/or may someday molest, rape, or, in some way, harm.

5. It is OK to murder full-term babies by cutting them piece by piece from their mother's womb.
6. What I feel trumps what is proven to be right.
7. We should be rewarded for our laziness.
8. You should be given everything even though you earned nothing, so you will keep voting for me.
9. It's all about me.
10. If I keep expanding the government, people will keep paying more unnecessary taxes, and things will never come crashing down in spite of what history proves.
11. If there is a God, I know more than Him.
12. God created us for our glory, not to glorify Him.
13. If we keep perverting the truth, there will be no consequences.
14. If we keep teaching stupidity, people will become smarter.
15. If we get them when they are young, we have them for good.
16. If we don't tell the parents of even the youngest schoolchildren, they won't find out.
17. If we get the media to support our gross immoralities, we can win this thing.
18. If we already have politicians and judges on our payroll, we can't lose.
19. If we can keep pastors and preachers from teaching the truths of the Bible, we have a fighting chance.
20. If we can intimidate pastors and preachers and threaten them with hate speech, they won't teach the truths of the Bible.
21. If we promote religions other than Christianity, even ones that promote the killing of Christians, Jews, and Americans, we can reach our goals of complete and total domination of the people.
22. We think we are gods; therefore, we are gods. If you don't think so, just ask us and we will tell you.

Well I hope by some of these, you can tell I am trying to get a point across. While the intelligent and knowledgeable and, dare I say, enlightened people of this country may not of actuality said some of these things, the things they do say, the laws they do pass, and the attitudes they do promote if followed down the road to a logical conclusion, where else could they be headed for?

Maybe them having absolute authority through governmental processes, which I think is a way of saying socialism or communism, is what they are after. I don't know, because I'm not intelligent or knowledgeable and definitely not enlightened. I'm just an over-taxed paying citizen trying to scrimp out a living for my wife and myself and hopefully have a little for our children and grandchildren when we are gone.

One more thing before I close this chapter. When will the leaders of this once great nation, again the so-called, or self-accredited by their actions, intelligent and knowledgeable people of this nation, see that prejudice is driving a great big wedge between the people? And it is the force behind so many of the perverted issues I brought up in this chapter.

I wonder if the people of color will realize that the forced promotion of their immoral values is harming children and in time will destroy this nation. By people of color, I don't mean red, yellow, brown, black, or white. I mean red, orange, yellow, green, blue, indigo, and violet, the rainbow flag followers who scream tolerance all the while being the most intolerant forcing their issues on everybody else.

I don't believe all intelligent and knowledgeable people support these disturbing lifestyles or their forced promotion, but to do nothing is the same as condoning their wickedness.

If you vote for politicians or send your children to schools of higher education or your alma mater that teach, foster, or promote these horrible ideologies, you are sponsoring the tragic end to our society and our culture. Whether that end comes through rebellion, judgment, or collapse of a government system fueled by greed and egos instead of common sense and following our constitution, we will have to wait and see. The way things are headed with immorality running rampant and morals and common sense and humility in such short supply it may not be too long.

My prayer is that we, as individuals, would seek forgiveness for our part of promoting and fostering a society that feels that so many of the disturbing things we teach are OK. That in seeking forgiveness, we would understand that there can be no forgiveness without repentance. And that without humility can there be true repentance.

Our God is faithful to forgive. Our Creator also knows the sincerity of our hearts and if we are truly sorry. So I pray that we would let go of our egos and surrender ourselves to the lover of our souls and seek His ways and His wisdom, for His honor and His glory.

CHAPTER 3

It is funny we want our food so clean, but the filthier our minds and our bodies, the better.

Well, welcome back. Let's see where this chapter ends up taking us. As you can probably tell, if you are still reading, I kind of start with a thought, and as I write, my mind is flooded with thoughts, so I don't really know what I am going to put on paper until it's on paper. I am so definitely not a writer.

The title for this chapter came about because of my work. As I mentioned before, I work in construction. I work for a company that erects premanufactured metal buildings. So I would be a premanufactured metal building erector. Yep, that's my job. As so many people have said over the years, "Oh it's like a big erector set!" Well yes, except you can't do it from the comfort of your living room, partly because we can't fit the big forklift in there, and we would get your couch dirty when we took our lunch break. For the younger readers (if there are any) who don't know what an erector set is, it was a toy way back when that had little metal pieces that you could bolt together with little tiny nuts and bolts to build different kinds of structures. I never had one, but I have been blessed to work for people who care about the quality of their work and the people who work for them. To find one of those qualities in an employer is rare these days, let alone both of them. Especially in the construction industry and even more so in our field.

A lot of our work is at processing plants and particularly almond processing plants. We don't put together machinery to process the nut. We put up the building to cover the machinery and protect the product being processed from outside elements.

It's amazing what they have to do in order to process their product. While I understand food processing areas need to be kept clean, it seems like with so many other things in our culture and society, the ones in the position of power are a bit power hungry and enjoy flexing their power muscles by making good people jump through unnecessary hoops, just to make themselves feel important.

At the plants, you have to sign in at the gate. Then, if you are not an employee, you need to sign in at the office and get a visitor tag. If you happen to be working in a processing area, which I believe is called a positive air pressure area, which means when you open a door and air blows out so allergens or bugs can't crawl in. They even have signs on doors that say, "No allergens beyond this point." My first thought was, who knew allergens could read (told you, I wasn't smart). Before you enter the processing area, you wash your hands, step onto a device that washes the bottom of your shoes, wash your hands again and apply some antibacterial lotion, and then you put a clean smock over your shirt. Oh and I forgot the hair, beard, and mustache nets. And that's just to work on something in the area, not to help process the nuts. They also have clean forklifts which stay only in the processing areas; they don't go outside. An outside lift brings the product to the speed door (which is a door that opens and closes real fast; don't worry, they all have safety features so no one gets hurt). Then the clean forklift brings it into the building. I am sure there are many more rules and regulations I don't know or care to know about, and if not, I'm sure there soon will be. I wonder how many millions, if not billions, of dollars are spent every year on only the cleanliness part of food processing.

It is truly amazing that any of us who has picked a nut, peach, pomegranate, apple, plumb, or any other fruit off a tree and rubbed it or washed grapes off in the canal we were swimming in and ate them is still alive.

Where I grew up, we had walnut and olive trees. My dad always got a kick out of getting some unsuspecting person to taste an unprocessed olive right off of the tree. They have a very bitter taste, and on a good day, he could get you to try it a second time by telling you, "Oh, you must have got a bad one. Here, try this one." It didn't matter who you were or how old you were, you were fair game if you were walking through the orchard with him. Amazingly, no one died.

A while back, the news was talking about a measles epidemic in California and the need for vaccinations. They said there were either twenty-three or fifty-three cases reported. With a population of over thirty-nine million, are twenty-three or fifty-three cases really an epidemic? When I was a kid, if my mom heard of someone she knew that kids had measles, mumps, or chicken pox, she would take us there hoping we would get whatever as a kid so we didn't get it as an adult. She was a nurse, so I suppose she knew what she was doing.

Nowadays, we have vaccinations for almost everything and are forced to get them all too often. While the vaccinations themselves may not be bad for us, I'm not sure, but all the things they put in them to make them work can't be healthy for our bodies and maybe for our mind. I have heard they put everything from heavy metals all the way to baby body parts in them. And the baby body parts have to be the harvested from aborted babies while they are still alive. I wonder who thinks it's a good idea to force these kinds of things into babies and children and the unsuspecting elderly and whoever else is led by the influence of the powers that be.

I believe our Creator, God, made our bodies to work and function without the need for so many of the medications or vaccines we have today. And He, in His imminent wisdom, has gifted some people at necessary times to invent some vaccine for a truly serious and devastating epidemic.

We, in our want it now and all about me society, no longer consume the nourishment that our bodies need to function properly. Instead, we pop a pill for this or that so we can feel like doing something, instead of doing something because it's the right thing to do. God created our bodies to get energy from the foods we eat. Nutrition leads to energy, energy leads to purpose, purpose leads to focus, focus leads to accomplishment, and accomplishment leads to true joy, if all is done with a focus on glorifying God.

Why is it that we spend billions on cleanliness for our foods, but when it comes to our minds, we spend billions making it the filthier, the better? When I was a kid, there were bra commercials on TV. The commercial I remember showed a mannequin top with no head, I think with a sweater on and a bra over the sweater, and a lady showing the benefits of the bra. Nowadays, you have live models strutting erotically down the runway in next to nothing. On prime time TV, you have women sitting on men in their beds, wearing almost nothing, just to advertise that particular show or TV series. Whoever came up with the slogan sex sells is probably a trillionaire by now. And the things they advertise with sex are unbelievable! Foods, clothes, cars, water, gum, shoes, body spray, and cologne, even animal rights organizations use sex to sell what they are selling, even though I'm not sure what that is. They even use sex to sell sexual aid products which might make sense, but not on primetime TV. Maybe late night if at all, but even their commercials are calm compared to some of these other products I mentioned. One that really bothers me is where they advertise for some sort of medication or drug that may help keep you from getting AIDS, and if you do get infected with AIDS, they have one, if taken quick enough, that may kill the virus in you. While these are good things, the way they advertise them promotes sex anywhere, anyway, any time, with anyone, not abstinence.

At church, the morning before I wrote this section, our pastor told us a story he had read in a book written by one of the best known evangelists of our time. The story was about a grandfather talking to his young grandson about there being two worlds inside each and every one of us. We have the world of right and goodness and doing things that honor God, warring continuously against the world of wrong and wretched and doing things that dishonor God. The grandson asked which world wins. The grandfather told him that the world you feed wins! I don't know if it was the evangelists and his grandfather talking or a story he was told, but he fed greatly the world that God used to do mighty things with his life.

You can plainly see what world our culture and society are feeding. A world full of filth, smut, sexual abuse, and the abuse of sex. We train young people to blow up people with video games and with TV programs all day long, and before they go out for the evening, we fill their desires full of sexual lust with commercials and TV programs that are on around the clock. It's no wonder why so many sports figures, music people, and Hollywood people struggle with some of these issues. Not only do we blow up their heads with tons of cash before they are weaned off of the filth and dirt in their minds from TV and other sources, but we also expect them to behave properly, when all they have been taught is an all about me attitude. It's not only famous people who struggle from the filth that is promoted by TV, movie executives, and business who pay big money to promote their products, but they are the ones we hear and read about in the news. It is plain and easy to see that greed is all that matters to these people. They could care less about how their sexual advertisement of a hamburger will affect an impressionable young boy or girl or how that same young awkward boy may truly believe (which is what the advertisers are hoping for) that all he has to do is buy this body spray and the girls will be all over him (which really doesn't point to anything intelligent about the mentality of the young women chasing after him just because he sprayed on some smelly stuff). Heck, sometimes it makes me wonder what if, and I didn't grow up with all this perverted crap on TV.

I got to ask the same question. Will all the young and older people led down the wrong path to death by some dreaded disease or in prison because of the sexual urges they couldn't contain due to explicit sexual television programs, reality shows, or television commercials that were forced on them while watching a primetime program, will these dead, diseased, or imprisoned people pass before the eyes of these TV executives and advertisers as they stand waiting for their final judgment before God who judges all for all of eternity?

When I was young, I remember cigarette and alcohol commercials all the time. Then the powers back then decided they were bad for our health and took them off of the TV. Now, they are back on TV. What happened? Did they all of a sudden become healthy, or did greed influence the decisions of the powers that be? I remember TV programs showing married couples in twin beds and full pajamas. Nowadays, you have silk sheets and skimpy lingerie clad actress straddling their partner and that's only the commercials. You can almost call them pornographic.

There were probably suggestive and somewhat racy ads when I was a kid, I don't remember, but then we only had three channels to choose from. Nowadays, there are hundreds.

Cigarettes and alcohol may be harmful to our physical health. But what about our mental health? Does it not matter as long as business and advertisers and TV and movie executives keep making their millions?

You may think I write like some dried up prudish old person mad because the good times have passed me by and because I can no longer enjoy the gifts God gives to us as a married man and wife, but you're wrong. And unfortunately, in these all about me days, I feel I need to clarify that married man and wife mean to each other (how sad is it that something like that needs clarification?). I worry because we no longer see sex as a gift, and like all true gifts that are given, they are to be treasured, appreciated, and enjoyed, not abused. And with this special intimate gift from our Creator, God, it is given to a married man and woman to enjoy in privacy and not in public or on TV to promote lust which sells products for a sick and disturbed society and fills the already overflowing prisons and pockets of the greedy money-focused instead of healthy mind-focused businesses and advertisers and TV and movie executives. Today, instead of being satisfied with the blessings they have been given, they keep upping the ante. One shows this so the other says that, all the while pushing the boundaries of filth and moral degradation simply to sell a product, which, in our simplemindedness and self-absorbedness, we follow like lambs to the slaughter.

With so many professions today in our society and culture, we adorn the most outlandish, rude, obnoxious, and promiscuous participants with the accolades. All the while, their behavior a few years back would have been deemed disgusting, revolting, or even illegal. But today, we publicize them, we idolize them, we make them our heroes, and we give them fortunes they don't appreciate. We bend over backward and even break laws to keep them out of jail and in front of audiences that pay big ticket prices to see the participants perform and buy the products that they may end up advertising someday down the road of fame and fortune. While I know this has always gone on with people from all walks of life, at least a few years back, they tried to keep it a secret and hidden from the public. Now, they wear it on their sleeves like a badge of honor. It seems that as long as the public is buying tickets to whatever event it may be, the participants and their promoters could care less on how sick and twisted and off the wall they get or how much money it may cost to get them out of trouble.

Owners of sports teams pay unbelievable amounts of money to a person who has been given the gift of throwing or hitting a ball, running or catching a ball, or bouncing a ball and putting it through a hoop. Owners complain about all the money. Ticket buyers complain about all the money the tickets cost to watch the events, yet everybody keeps paying the money. I enjoy watching sports and movies on TV and listening to music on the radio, but I do believe it is way out of hand. And like I mentioned about our national debt earlier, it will take big steps to make little changes, and as long as owners and advertisers don't care about anything other than being number one, and we keep paying higher and higher ticket prices and more and more for refreshments at events we choose to promote, things won't change; they will only get more and more out of control.

These participants, whether in sports, movies, music, or TV, or any other likewise professions, all they do is entertain. They don't heal people. They don't feed people. They don't give care to people. They don't shelter people. They don't protect people. They don't teach people (other than through their influence we may see on TV or hear about on the news, good or bad).

Why should some sports figure blessed with speed and agility or some singer blessed with a nightingale voice be paid so much money? It's not like they can perform a lifesaving operation after years of schooling and practice. Do they plow fields or milk cows to provide food and nourishment for the masses? Do they board by board build houses to protect people from the harshness of society and weather? Do they risk their lives protecting people? No! They only entertain us. So why do we allow them to make so much for so little? We buy high-priced tickets to see them perform and buy the products they are paid to advertise, because it is all about me! How I want to feel, how I think I should feel, and whatever it takes to make me feel the way I believe I should feel no matter what my circumstances may dictate.

I remember several years ago seeing for the first time rims on a car that when you stopped they didn't, they kept spinning. They cost lots of money. I remember seeing parked on the grass in the front yard of a tiny rundown house a fancy car with these fancy expensive spinning rims on it. I thought that the car was probably worth more than the house. I wondered why someone would live in a tiny rundown house but have such an expensive vehicle. While I know it was none of my business nor was it my problem, I wondered what kind of influence that this person had to make this kind of choice. Did they care more a about what people who didn't know them thought about them than what their family lived in?

As you look around, you see a look at me mentality rapidly expanding in our culture and society. We can also see a look at me mentality or anything for my fifteen minutes of fame, eroding the foundation of our county.

So many of the political leaders have given in to the all about me mentality. I wish I could say it is only younger elected officials, but so many of the older ones also promote an all about me mentality. They may deny it, but if they promote abortion, welfare, and free college, to name only a few things, or if they promote a socialists type of government to keep themselves in power and you vote for them, you don't want to work for and earn the rewards you get; you want them taken from someone who has earned them and given to you without any effort on your part. And we are too lazy and too stupid to see where that road leads even though there is plenty of evidence of fallen governments to teach the truth. Many of these leaders build fortunes protecting the industries that are tearing down and destroying our country, but they don't care as long as they get their due (which they will when judgment day comes "knocking"). They have promoted, passed, and protected laws that tear apart the family, all for their personal gain.

The family is the back bone of this country. Our founding fathers fought, died, and used their own resources to rescue their own and other families from the sickness that had infected the leaders of their previous culture and society. And now that same sickness has infected so many of the leaders of our culture and society, and it is in epidemic proportions.

If the so-called knowledgeable and intelligent people want to do some good for a change, maybe they could put their heads together and come up with a vaccine to cure the self-absorbed, all about me attitude and mentality that is and has been promoted in this country for way too many years now. And maybe they could throw in some get off the couch and get a job or maybe a little (or a lot) of humbleness, truthfulness, thankfulness, gratefulness, kindness, gentleness, and some honesty. Sincerity wouldn't hurt either.

Again, I wonder where they see this going. The social media outlets publicizing and promoting such issues as abortion, LGBT issues, unlimited undocumented immigration, and higher education for all at no cost and promoting religions or ideologies other than the faith that founded this once great nation, even as some of these are sneaking in the front doors of our school systems to indoctrinate our youngest of children to their unholy ways of thinking.

When all these media giants win or get what they want, backed by the politicians they have sponsored, do they honestly believe that this nation will remain a nation that fosters, promotes, or even allows someone like themselves to build a product like theirs to grow their business to the force they have become? If they get what they want, no one will be working to buy their products because they have censored the people who keep growing business and who employ people who purchase their products. Your business, like our government, will implode when you have more money out go than income. If you keep promoting through your censorship a socialist's form of government, who will control your business, them? If you have profit, will they also take that to support the government you helped create, because so many people are given the freebies? And if that isn't enough, will they also take your accumulated wealth? After all, you did support the share the wealth socialist's way of life. Or did you think they would only take what little wealth the middle class working people had scrimped and saved for hopefully a more relaxed and rewarding retirement?

What other countries have created the technologies that have been created here in the United States? And of the ones created elsewhere, how many of them have become billionaires or are their government leaders profiting instead of them?

How foolish and ignorant are any of us to think that we can destroy a government system for the people and by the people guided by the hand of God and that there will be no consequences. You can foolishly promote and legislate other faiths or ideologies into power, but that does not change the fact that God our Creator is still in control. You can take prayer out of schools and allow prayer rugs and sexual perversions to take its place. You can have drag queens groom young children at county or city libraries for their own sick pleasures. You can continue to force your sick perversions onto those of us who have stepped out of darkness and deception and have surrendered to the light of Jesus Christ, but that will never change the fact that they are disgustingly wrong and terribly misguided.

Common sense and science say there are two genders.

Emotion says as many sexual preferences as we want, and we will label them genders to make ourselves feel better.

Common sense and science say life begins at inception.

Greed and prejudices say life begins when we say it does as long as we can make a buck off of it.

God, common sense, and science say that God created everything and that He created it all from nothing.

Evolutionists say that we evolved from molten matter and our government and school systems have adopted and promoted this lie even though there is no proof.

Our great God is and always has been in control. The Bible teaches that He desires that none should perish. That He is long suffering and patient. The Bible is full of times when He waited for a change of heart in His chosen people. But it didn't happen, so He sent in a pagan nation to discipline them. After years of slavery and punishment, they repented of their sin as a nation and cried out to God for mercy and to rescue them.

God gives us His truth. Anything contrary to His truth is a lie and, therefore, is sin. He gives us His truth for our own good. He created us, so He knows what's best for us. He desired that we all would come to Him and His truth. It is His truth that saves us from the fires of hell and suffering for all eternity. Desiring to live for Him in His truth, not surrendering to Satan and his lies about our feelings and emotions, is what brings us to the foot of Jesus, the cross, and our own individual salvation.

My prayer is that we, as individuals and corporately as a nation, would surrender ourselves to the truth of the Word of God. That in surrendering ourselves, our perspectives and our ways of thinking and understanding would be changed. That the shame and guilt of our humanity would be overcome by our obedience and surrendering to the suffering of our Lord and Savior on the cross. That through His suffering, and our surrendering, obedience, and repentance, we may find true joy, true peace, and true freedom. And that when we as individuals are called home for judgment before our great God, we would be found pure and blameless because of the blood shed by our Lord and Savior, Jesus Christ.

Thank you, Father

I Love You
Scott

CHAPTER 4

Before It's too Late

Well, here it is the last chapter of this book, if it ever becomes one that is. Some of you are saying oh thank goodness. Some are hopefully not so elated (i.e., if anyone has seen or heard of this book besides a couple of people). Remember, I am writing in what I believe and hope is in obedience to the God of all creation and judge of all eternity. So this book, if it does become one, may be short and scattered and even confusing at times and for sure irritating to so many if not all, you liberal and progressive thinkers. I believe it is written to you more than anyone else. Your feelings and your emotions which leads to your ways of thinking, leading to your attitudes and your actions which then leads to the influence you have on others and to so many of the atrocities that we now condone and promote and profit from and even pass laws to protect as a nation.

I wish I could say it is because of ignorance or stupidity, but science says there are only two genders and life begins at conception, studies have proven that children do better when raised by their mothers and their fathers, and history has demonstrated time and time again that when you promote welfare and free giveaway programs, governmental collapse is soon to follow. There are tons of evidence disproving what you, liberal and progressive-thinking people, feel to be right. So it is not a problem of proof; it is a problem of the heart. Of what you feel and how you let your emotions rule over your common sense. So it can't be ignorance! As far as stupidity goes, so many of you are either teaching or are being taught this foolishness in higher learning institutions so you can't be stupid! I do not doubt for a moment that you, people, are sincere, but I do believe with all my heart that you are sincerely wrong.

No child of any age, let alone starting in kindergarten, should be taught about sex, let alone anal sex, sex with sex toys, and, if you can't afford to buy sex toys, a list of fruits or vegetables that could be used instead. We have school authorities promoting and forcing sex and gender issues onto our children and being backed by governmental agencies that threaten to take our children away if we as parents don't conform to their sick ways of thinking. We have transsexuals sharing story time at our libraries, grooming young innocent children.

Yet try bringing your Bible to school or praying at a graduation or a sports event and see what kind of trouble you get into. You, people, even want to spread this filth by controlling what is taught at the homes of people who have chosen to homeschool their own children in an attempt to escape the filth you call education.

This nation was founded by our founding fathers at great cost to themselves. They gave life and limbs and fortunes to secure freedom for all. All includes everyone including all you, liberal and progressive thinkers, gays and lesbians, transgendered, and LGBT-minded people. All also includes all of us who don't identify or agree with the lifestyles you have chosen to live. Yet we don't persecute you, bankrupt your company, or throw you into jail because you won't promote or condone our lifestyle choices. It seems freedom to you means something different than it does to me. To me, it means live and let live. I don't agree with many things and many people. Sometimes I don't agree with the people I love the most; sometimes we have different opinions on certain things. That doesn't mean I am going to do violent things against them, like we see on so many higher learning campuses these days when liberal students don't like the thoughts or opinions of more conservative students.

I want to be free to live my life as I choose. And as long as my choices don't infringe on anyone else's freedom, I should be allowed to do so. Now I'm not foolish enough to think that I am perfect and that my choices will never conflict with someone else's choices. That is where compromise comes into play. I and most people make compromises all the time. When we can't compromise, then laws come into play. I do not wish to force my freedom to believe and trust in Jesus Christ as not only the Creator and sustainer of the universe but also as the one and only Savior of the world, onto everyone else, but I do, through the freedom given to me by the constitution of the United States, have the right to share my faith and my beliefs, just as you who believe differently have the right to share. My question then to you, liberal and progressive politicians, leaders, judges, lawyers, professors, and thinkers, is why do you feel or think you have the right to force your beliefs, ideologies, ungodly morals, and ways of life onto those of us who believe differently? I am OK with you living your lifestyle. When your judgment day arrives, it may not bode well for you though, but that is your choice given to you first by God and then by the constitution of the United States.

Why do you feel it necessary to force your chosen lifestyles onto the rest of us, even the innocent children that you are trying to indoctrinate? Do you believe that if laws are passed and people are forced to accept your ways of thinking, it will somehow make it OK or right? I'm sorry, it won't. Sin is sin no matter how hard we may try to justify it. No matter how many laws are passed and lives are lost to these perversions, truth is truth, right is right, and wrong is wrong, and God has told us which is which in the Bible. You may say you believe in a different god or no god at all. That is your right given to you by God and the constitution of the United States. But it does not change the evidence, and the evidence points to God of the Bible. It does not point to evolution or the other gods of other religions or reincarnation. While we have been given the right or freedom to choose, we will be held accountable for our choices. Here on earth, we may escape jail or judgment for our wrong doings, but our eternal destinations will be determined by the choices we have made and the attitudes of our hearts, and no lies, laws, or fast talking will change the outcome, and judgment is forever, no commuted sentences, no time off for good behavior, just eternal torment.

I have heard hell described something like this. From the day of your birth, you suffer terribly from the worse things you can imagine. Your whole life is lived in suffering and pain. Upon your death and first seconds after being delivered to hell, it will make your existence on earth seem like a wonderful life, a party.

I have heard heaven described something like this. From the day of your birth, you are given every wonderful thing you could ever imagine. Only great and wonderful things happen for you. Upon your death and first seconds after arriving in heaven, your life on earth will seem like hell.

Have you given any thought of where you will spend your eternity? Which do you prefer, heaven or hell? Those are your only two choices. You are not reincarnated, you will not become a god of your own planet, and there will not be seventy black-eyed virgins waiting for you. If you choose suffering and torment, keep on protecting, promoting, and profiting from such horrific things like abortion, destruction of the family, and all the sexual perversions you are trying to force everyone else to accept. In short, just keep on living the worldly focused life you are living. If you choose heaven, know that you must be perfect and sinless. Are you perfect and sinless? If your answer from your heart is no, then you, like every single one of us, need a savior. It is Christ's perfect righteousness that opens the gates to heaven, for us. It is the blood He shed on His cross at Calvary for our salvation. He alone is the Savior of the world. He alone is perfect, and He alone is capable of paying our sins' debt and making us acceptable.

Have you ever given any thought of the fact that God spoke the universe into existence along with everything in it? He created it all from nothing. He spoke, and there it was. But for our salvation, He had to send His sinless Son to a horrible death on the cross.

Well, if it's not ignorance or stupidity, then how can we explain the fact that so many smart and intelligent people, so many of the politicians, so many of the judges and lawyers, so many of the Hollywood-type people, and so many other wealthy and influential people condone, support, and promote such sinful foolishness? Why is it that in areas where these influential people live and work, homelessness problems are so big? One would think that with all their wealth and supposed care about those homeless people, areas like

Los Angeles and San Francisco would have no homeless people at all. But they are flooded with homeless people and issues which are only getting bigger and bigger. And how do they propose to fix their homelessness problems? They believe that if they let undocumented homeless people from other countries come here with open borders, that will evidently fix the problems of the homeless people in our country. You might think that that is foolish and stupid. And they don't believe it will fix our homeless problem. Then I ask you, why do they condemn our sitting president for trying to protect their and our country from the financial burden of providing care for many more homeless and welfare recipients when we are already struggling to take care of the homeless and welfare situation we have? Not to mention the terrorists and drugs that sneak or are snuck across the open borders.

I see you, actors, on your award shows cussing and making obscene jesters toward our president. At least he is trying to maintain the issues we already have, and all you can do is demean and make up lies about him and what he is trying to do. Now, maybe an out of control government and out of control spending by an expanding government which leads to out of control taxation isn't a problem for you, with all your millions, but for me, a middle class working person, it makes it very hard to make ends meet, and I don't have a home, let alone a mansion on each coast, and who knows how many others.

Same old question. How do you see all this ending? And maybe more import, who do you see paying for it all? Evidently, you, liberal and progressive types, aren't going to because it seems worse where you live. But that's OK. Let all those undocumented people, good and bad people, come into this country so you can keep your liberal and progressive politicians in power and then maybe when you don't have a pot to piss in, that will open your eyes to your emotional way of thinking and politicking. Why don't all you, people, put your millions where your mouth and obscene gestures are and help the homeless in your own areas? And all you, liberal politicians, who have acquired millions from a job that pays only thousands, help the homeless in your areas? Or does it make you feel important or like the kings and queens you feel you should be when you hand out crumbs to these homeless people in your areas?

Your liberal and progressive attitudes which lead to your liberal and progressive ways of thinking, which again leads to your liberal and progressive actions and then to your destructive liberal and progressive influence, make me wonder if you hate our country. You, liberal and progressive politicians, now running for president want to destroy this country, either by financial collapse, with all your welfare and green issues and healthcare and higher learning for everyone. Yet I have not heard of how you, people, intend to pay for all these tax-funded giveaway programs. Maybe you will dig into your big bank accounts and throw a little into the pot (I doubt it). Oh, that's right, you will tax the rich. Well from where I sit, you and your cronies are the rich. Or maybe you mean the really, really rich. I wonder if any of your Hollywood supporters fall into your category of rich and will be taxed excessively to support all your programs. If I was a rich businessman and you came after what I worked hard to acquire for my family and myself to pay for all your welfare programs, I might just cut my losses, shut down my business, and see if I can benefit from any of your tax-funded free programs. Sometimes, enough is enough, but lines will be long because all the people I used to employ will be there also.

You, people, want to create a weaker nation. You want our military service to be greatly downsized. Maybe that's where you will get some of the money to pay for your free giveaway programs. And maybe that's how you want to destroy this nation, by being overthrown by another government because you have greatly weakened our protective forces. And, on top of that, have taken guns away from sane law-abiding citizens who now can't protect their families from foreign governments or possibly from our government that has become power hungry and no longer even tries to govern aided by the constitution of the United States but by a small group of liberal and progressive so-called leaders. Maybe that's how you want to destroy our nation.

Maybe you will destroy this nation by forcing your unhealthy and perverse ways of thinking about the value of human life or in your cases the valuelessness of human life onto the people you were elected to protect. Our president is trying to protect the people he swore to protect, and you, liberal and progressive types, fight him every step of the way. You search for issues to bring him down, and when you can't find any, you make them up and spend millions upon millions of our tax dollars trying to deceive the American people into believing he is some kind of a monster. He is trying to protect unborn babies and full-term babies from being cut piece by piece from their mother's womb, and you want him to be perceived as some kind of a monster. Maybe you, liberal and progressive types, should take a good long look into a mirror. He is trying to protect our children he swore to protect from drugs, sex offenders, sex traffickers, and terrorists from coming across our unprotected borders, and you fight him tooth and nail, when many, if not most, of these people could be kept away from our children if you would give him the small amount of our tax money it would take to build the wall you already OK'd but didn't build because it would threaten your liberal and progressive political careers. But instead, you will spend our tax money forcing your perverted views of sex onto our children, even the youngest ones, and funding organizations that promote and perform abortions. Maybe that's why you want to take our guns away, because you know how mixed or messed up the next generation will be because of all the sick and perverted things you, liberal and progressive types, are forcing them to learn at schools. How can they know right from wrong when they can't even decide if they are a boy or a girl, because you have forced confusion into their young minds? That along with your hate for unborn life, it's no wonder we have so many people going on shooting rampages. Why should they value human life when the liberal and progressive leaders of their own country pass laws to promote, protect, and even profit from the murdering of the most innocent of people. I wonder when you, liberal and progressive politicians and leaders, will start passing laws to protect and profit from murder. Oh, wait, you already do. You just call it a woman's right to choose. Why don't we pass laws to help people choose abstinence? Oh, wait, you can't profit from abstinence! Which means you can't give kickbacks. Oh, silly me!

You who keep voting these liberal and progressive politicians into office, where do you think you will stand when they bankrupt our nation? With all their costly free giveaway programs, whose government-sponsored paycheck will go away first, yours or theirs? Whose tax-funded government-sponsored healthcare will go away first, your basic care or their plush healthcare program? You who are for the share the wealth instead of earn it for yourself programs, where do you think you will stand when there is no more wealth to share because you voted for people who gave it all away until there is no more wealth to give? Do you really think those politicians you helped put into a place of power will share their wealth with you? They aren't stupid. Yes, maybe greedy and self-absorbed, but they knew exactly what they were doing when they deceived you into voting for them. To know how all this will work out if the liberal and the progressive types get their way, just look back into history. This story has been written time and time again.

The only hope we have as a nation to survive is to turn away from our wickedness and elect politicians and judges who believe and desire to follow the constitution of the United States. Leaders who have faith in God of the Bible and are governed by the constitution, not by their feeling and/or their emotions.

Our country has been a care giver and big brother to many countries who need help from disaster or devastation or protection from horrific tragedies inflicted on them from their own leaders. We are becoming weaker and weaker because of so much unwise leadership and legislation, being and that has been passed for way too many years now. For so many years now, we have been tearing down the foundation that has made this country strong. We need to look back at history to see what made us the country that sets the standards for the rest of the world and start coming together and passing laws to protect everyone, not only the few. To look at the constitution that has lasted longer than any other constitution of any country in history.

We need to seek out what is right, not only what we feel is right. Someone may feel it is right to go into a school and start shooting. If that same person had been taught what is truly right and not led by his or her feeling and emotions and the confusion which often accompanies emotional decision-making, these kinds of tragedies may cease to exist. I don't recall as a kid hearing about these kinds of terrible things happening. Maybe because we were taught right is right and wrong is wrong and understood that blessing or consequences would follow each decision we made. Maybe our society and culture and government fifty plus years ago focused more on the people as a united nation, and, therefore, people focused more on others than on one's self. We were not so self-absorbed and self-important. We were taught reading, writing, arithmetic, spelling (which if you could have read this before editing, you could tell I flunked), history, and health. And not the perverted health you pass into laws to force onto our tiny children.

I remember sex education in sixth grade. Boys went into the cafeteria and watched a film on the projector. It taught us about hygiene and cleanliness and that we may start growing hair in places we never had it before. Oh, and that it is easier to trim your fingernails and toenails after a bath or shower and that you may need to start using deodorant. That's it. No sexual positions or suggestions on which gender you are or could become if you desired to and no advice on which sex toy might work best for you! All these kinds of things kids will learn way to soon anyways, so why do the knowledgeable and intelligent people believe this perversion needs to be forced on them starting in kindergarten? Then our foolish liberal and progressive politicians force legislation and pass laws to force their filth onto our babies.

So what's next? How far down the ladder of degradation will we climb, in the name of equal rights? How far from destruction of this country, whether financial or by terrorist or by self-destruction or judgment, are we willing to go?

Many people and many of our leaders, political or otherwise, think they can legislate God out of office. You, foolish people, believe you can impeach the God of all creation? You may pass legislation and bit by bit try to force Him out of the lives of His chosen ones, but to think even for a nanosecond that He will cease to be the God of all creation is total idiocy on your part. Do you truly believe you can pass legislation and again the God of all creation will cease to exist? I believe that as the book of Romans chapter 1 verse 28 says, God gave them over to a debased mind to do the things which are not fitting. I am going to end now, but I will leave you with the Bible verses from Romans 1 verses 18–32, so in case you don't have a Bible, you can know that the God you may think has no power or does not exist knew that you would be where you are right now, on the verge of eternal damnation.

God's Wrath on Unrighteousness

> For the wrath of God is revealed from heaven against all ungodliness and unrighteousness of men, who suppress the truth in unrighteousness because what may be known of God is manifest in them, for God has shown it to them. For since the creation of the world His invisible attributes are clearly seen, being understood by the things that are made, even His eternal power and God Head, so that they are without excuse, because, although they knew God, they did not glorify Him as God, nor were thankful, but became futile in their thoughts, and their foolish hearts were darkened. Professing to be wise, they became fools. And changed the glory of the incorruptible God into an image made like corruptible man—and birds and four—footed animals and creeping things.
>
> Therefore God also gave them up to uncleanness, in the lusts of their hearts, to dishonor their bodies among themselves, who exchanged the truth of God for the lie, and worshipped and served the creature rather than the Creator, who is blessed forever. Amen.
>
> For this reason God gave them up to vile passions. For even their women exchanged the natural use for what is against nature. Likewise

> also the men, leaving the natural use of the woman, burned in their lust for one another, men with men committing what is shameful, and receiving in themselves the penalty of their error which was due.
>
> And even as they did not like to retain God in their knowledge, God gave them over to a debased mind, to do those things which are not fitting; being filled with all unrighteousness, sexual immorality, wickedness, covetousness, maliciousness; full of envy, murder, strife, deceit, evil-mindedness; they are whisperers, backbiters, haters of God, violent, proud, boasters, inventors of evil things, disobedient to parents, undiscerning, untrustworthy, unloving, unforgiving, unmerciful, who knowing the righteous judgment of God, that those who practice such things are deserving of death, not only do the same but also approve of those who practice them. (Romans 1:18–32)

My Prayer

Our great and all powerful and ever-present God, please, I pray, open all of our eyes individually and corporately as a nation to Your truth before it is entirely too late. Open our eyes to see your wrath of abandonment by removing your restraints and allowing the people of this nation to go to their sin wholeheartedly and the consequences that will soon follow. I pray we will turn away from our sins and back to You, oh God. We will cry out to You for forgiveness of all our sins and seek guidance back to You, Your will, and Your way for our lives and our nation before You give us over completely to a debased mind with no hope of eternal salvation, only eternal damnation.

Thank You

I Love You
Scott

ABOUT THE AUTHOR

Scott Johnsen states that he is not a writer, but he is a sinner saved by the grace of God. He has worked in construction since before he graduated from high school, around forty-five years. Scott grew up on a small farm. He is married with three children and five grandchildren. He worries about not only their future but also where they will spend their eternal life.

CPSIA information can be obtained
at www.ICGtesting.com
Printed in the USA
LVHW042257200523
747592LV00019B/274

9 781644 688403